Counting 1 to 10

1

2

3

4

5

6

7

8

9

10

Trace the Number 1

To Parents: Following the arrow, trace the number 1 with your finger and say "one." Guide your child's hand to help them trace the number. Then, encourage your child to try tracing alone.

  Trace the number 1 and say "one."

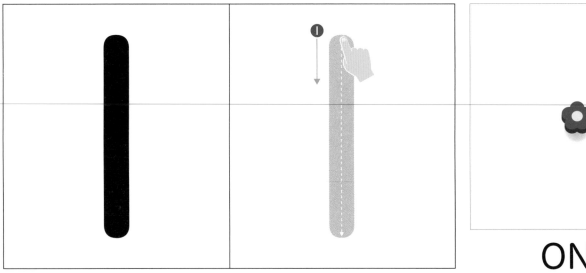

ONE

 Color the balloon. Say "one balloon."

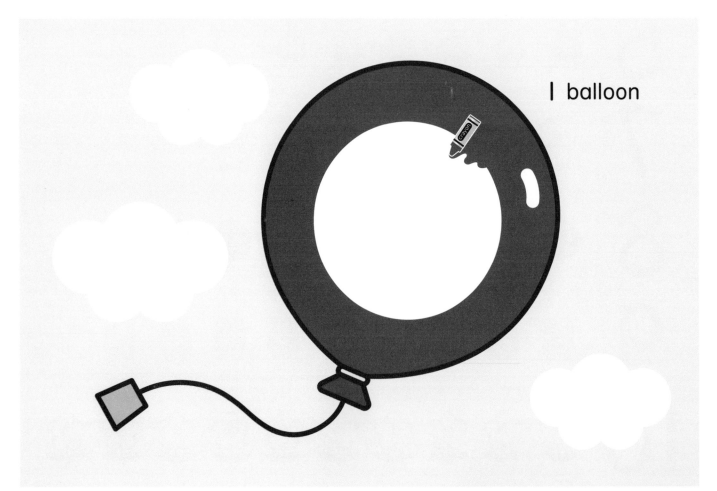

1 balloon

Let's Count

To Parents: Demonstrate how to stand like the bear in the picture to make your body look like the number 1. Encourage your child to try it too!

Sticker
Good job!

 Turn your body into the number 1, and say "One!"

One!

One!

1 bear

Trace the Number 2

To Parents: Following the arrow, trace the number 2 with your finger and say "two." Guide your child's hand to help them trace the number. Then, encourage them to trace alone. Have your child press their pointer finger on each object when counting to make it a habit.

  Trace the number 2 and say "two."

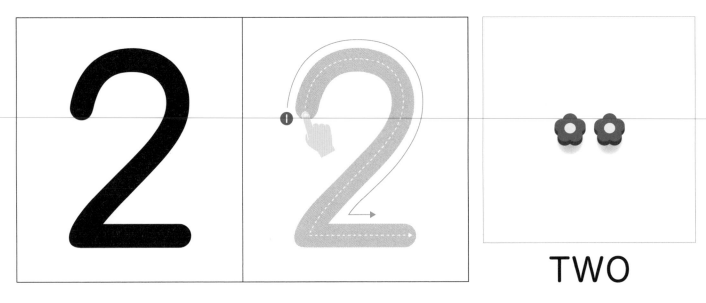

TWO

 Finish coloring the 2 excavators. Count them: "One, two."

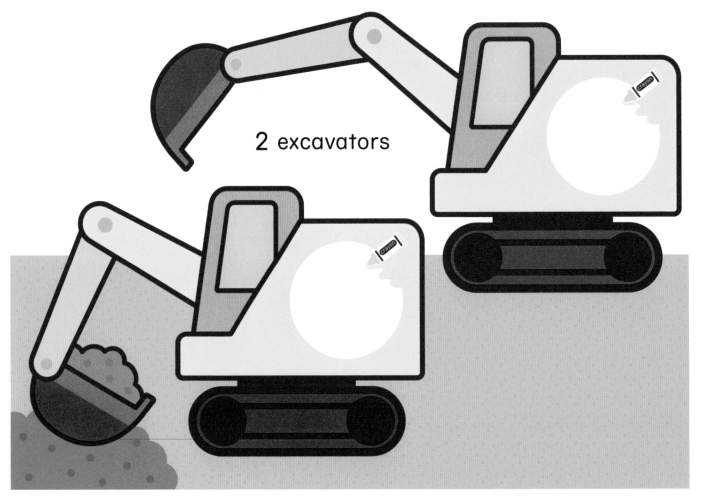

2 excavators

Let's Count

To Parents: Give your child the two bus stickers provided and encourage them to place the stickers on their shadows in the picture. Count together: "One, two. Two buses. Vroom vroom."

 Put the bus stickers on their shadows. Then, trace the path from ➡ to ➡ and say "two."

2 buses

Trace the Number 3

To Parents: Following the arrow, trace the number 3 with your finger and say "three." Guide your child's hand to help them trace the number. Then, encourage them to trace alone. Have your child press their pointer finger on each object when counting to make it a habit.

  Trace the number 3 and say "three."

THREE

 Finish coloring the 3 carrots. Count them: "One, two, three."

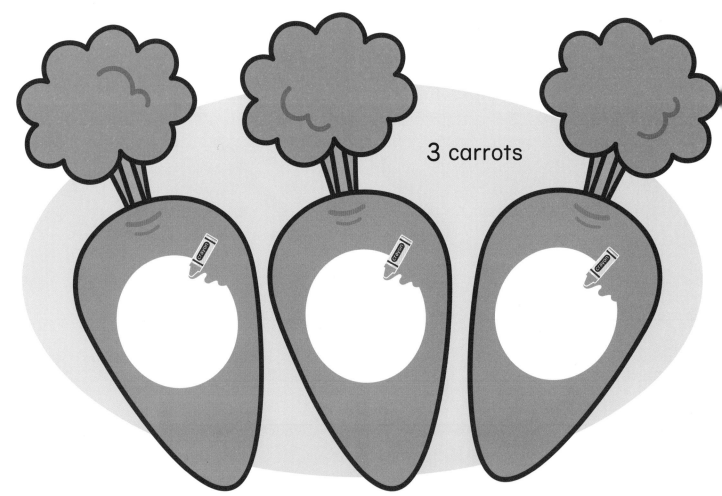

3 carrots

Let's Count

To Parents: Once you've provided 3 smiley face stickers, say to your child, "There are three rabbits. Look at the carrots on page 6. There are also three of them." It's important to confirm that there is the same number of the different objects.

Good job!

   Put a 😊 sticker on each rabbit. Count them. Then, find the number 3.

3 rabbits

Trace the Number 4

To Parents: Following the arrows, trace the number 4 with your finger and say "four." Guide your child's hand to help them trace the number. Then, encourage them to trace alone. Have your child press their pointer finger on each object when counting to make it a habit.

 Trace the number 4 and say "four."

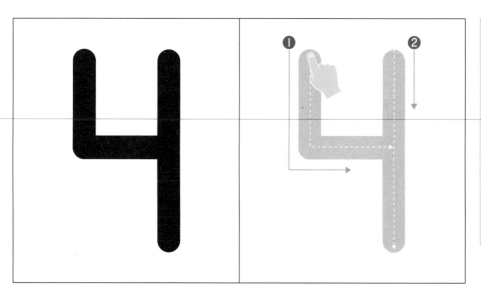

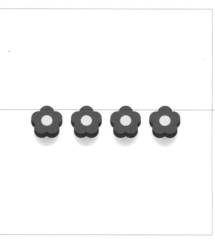

FOUR

 Finish coloring the 4 stars. Count them: "One, two, three, four."

4 stars

Let's Count

To Parents: Give your child the animal stickers provided and let them place the stickers on the rocket ship in any order.

  Place 1 animal sticker in each window of the rocket ship.
Then, find the number 4.

4 animals

Trace the Number 5

To Parents: Following the arrows, trace the number 5 with your finger and say "five." Guide your child's hand to help them trace the number. Then, encourage them to trace alone. Have your child press their pointer finger on each object when counting to make it a habit.

 Trace the number 5 and say "five."

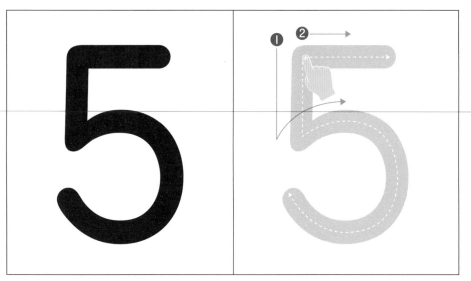

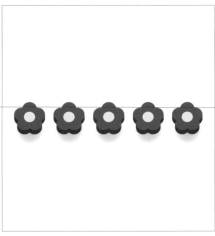

FIVE

 Finish coloring the 5 fish. Count them: "One, two, three, four, five."

5 fish

Let's Count

To Parents: Give your child the banana stickers provided. After they place the stickers in the gorilla's mouth, ask, "How many bananas is the gorilla eating? Let's count them together: one, two, three, four, five."

  Put the banana stickers in the gorilla's mouth and count them. Then, find the number 5.

5 bananas

Make Pairs

Draw a line to connect each child with 1 sundae.

example

Make Pairs

To Parents: Together, count the numbers of bees. Then, count the tulips. Ask, "Are they the same number"? Encourage your child to draw lines to connect a bee with a tulip. Do you have any pairs of shoes or socks nearby? Use them to further illustrate to your child how items can be matched into pairs.

 Draw a line to connect each bee with 1 tulip.

example

Use on page 14.

glue glue glue

Complete the Picture

To Parents: Cut the animals along the solid gray line. Then, apply glue to the back of each picture and give them to your child. Let your child place the animals in the boxes on the train. Count the animals aloud together.

 Paste the animals onto the picture so they can ride the train. Then, count them.

Parents: Cut out the animals for your child.

Complete the Picture

To Parents: Together, count the cars on the ride. Then, count the stickers provided for this page. Encourage your child to put each animal in a separate car while counting to 5.

Put animal stickers on each window of the Ferris wheel.

Make Things Equal

To Parents: Ask your child to try to keep things equal when drawing sauce and adding the provided fork stickers.

  Draw an equal amount of sauce on each dish. Then, add a fork sticker to each plate.

example

Make Pairs

To Parents: Ask your child to count the cupcakes and plates on this page. Then, ask them to make 3 pairs by drawing lines to connect each cupcake to each plate. Cut the solid gray line. Encourage your child to fold the page to show the cupcakes on the plates.

  Draw a line to connect each cupcake with I dish.
Then, fold the page to show the cupcakes on the plates!

How to Play

Fold up

example

Parents: Cut along the gray line for your child.

Look and Find

To Parents: Start by asking your child to name the vehicles. Provide a smiley-face sticker for the fire truck. Ask your child, "How many fire trucks are there?" Together, count all 5 vehicles.

 Put a sticker on the fire truck.

Look and Find

To Parents: Start by asking your child to name the vehicles. Provide 2 smiley face stickers for the police cars. Ask your child, "How many police cars are there?"

 Find 2 police cars. Put stickers on them.

Count the Frogs

To Parents: First, count the frogs. Then, cut the page for your child. Encourage your child to fold the page and say "three, three frogs." Ask them to name what they see as they fold and unfold the page (example : three frogs, the number 3).

  Count the frogs. Then, fold along the --- and —–— lines for a surprise!

How to Play

Fold up

3 frogs

Fold down

Parents: Cut along the gray line for your child.

Count the Chicks

To Parents: First, count the chicks. Then, cut the page for your child. Encourage your child to fold the page and say "four, four chicks." Ask them to name what they see as they fold and unfold the page (example : four chicks, the number 4).

  Count the chicks. Then, fold along the --- and ——— lines for a surprise!

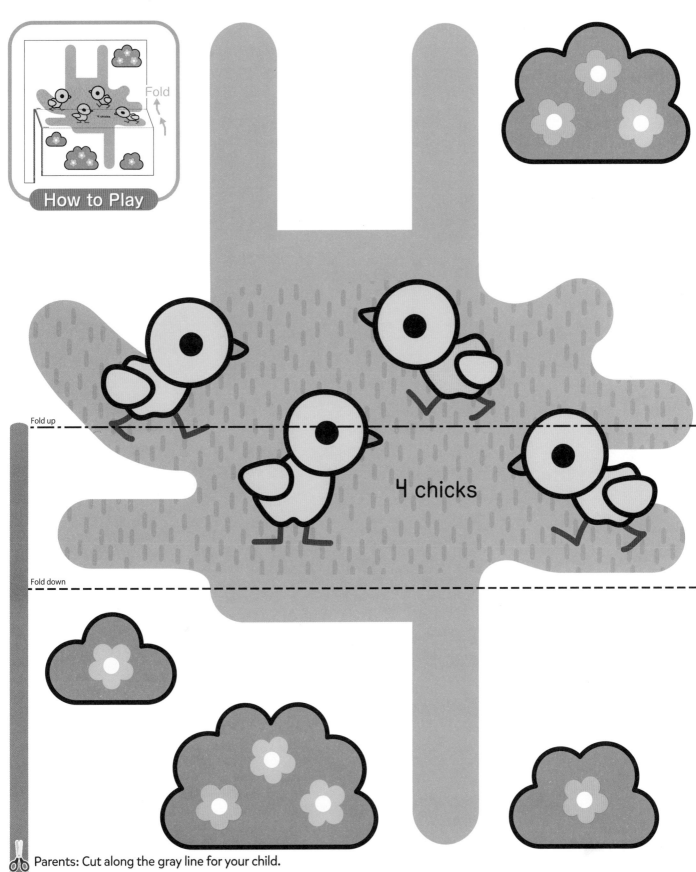

How to Play

Fold

Fold up

Fold down

4 chicks

Parents: Cut along the gray line for your child.

Count the Pumpkins

To Parents: First, count the pumpkins. Then, cut the page for your child. Encourage your child to fold the page and say "five, five pumpkins." Ask them to name what they see as they fold and unfold the page (example : five pumpkins, the number 5).

  Count the pumpkins. Then, fold along the --- and ––– lines for a surprise!

How to Play

Fold down

5 pumpkins

Fold up

Match the Numbers

To Parents: This activity focuses on connecting numbers and objects. If your child has difficulty recognizing the numbers 3 and 4, count the fruits together. Ask your child how many pears there are and help them draw a line from the pears to the number 4.

 Draw a line to connect each number with the amount of fruit it matches.

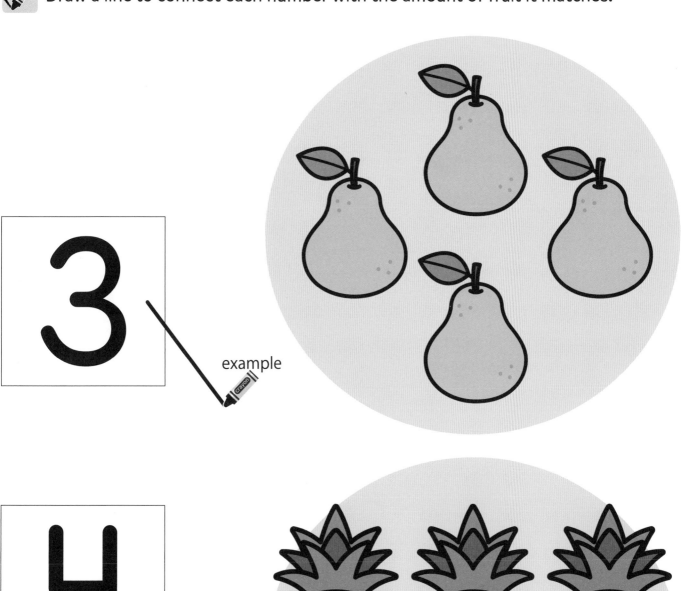

example

Match the Numbers

To Parents: Have your child point to each animal as they count. If needed, count together. If your child has difficulty recognizing the numbers, write down the number you counted.

 Count the animals. Then, color the circle below the number that matches the number of animals in the picture.

2 | **5**

example

l | **3**

Match the Numbers

To Parents: Have your child point to each animal as they count. If needed, count together. If your child has difficulty recognizing the numbers, write down the number you counted.

 Count the animals. Then, color the circle below the number that matches the number of animals in the picture.

Trace and Match

To Parents: Encourage your child to trace the number I with a finger, then with a crayon. Count the dinosaurs in each piece of art to determine which matches the number I. Be sure to ask, "Which piece of art has one dinosaur?" Ask them to draw a line to the picture with I dinosaur.

Trace the number I and say "one." Then, draw a line to I dinosaur.

ONE

example

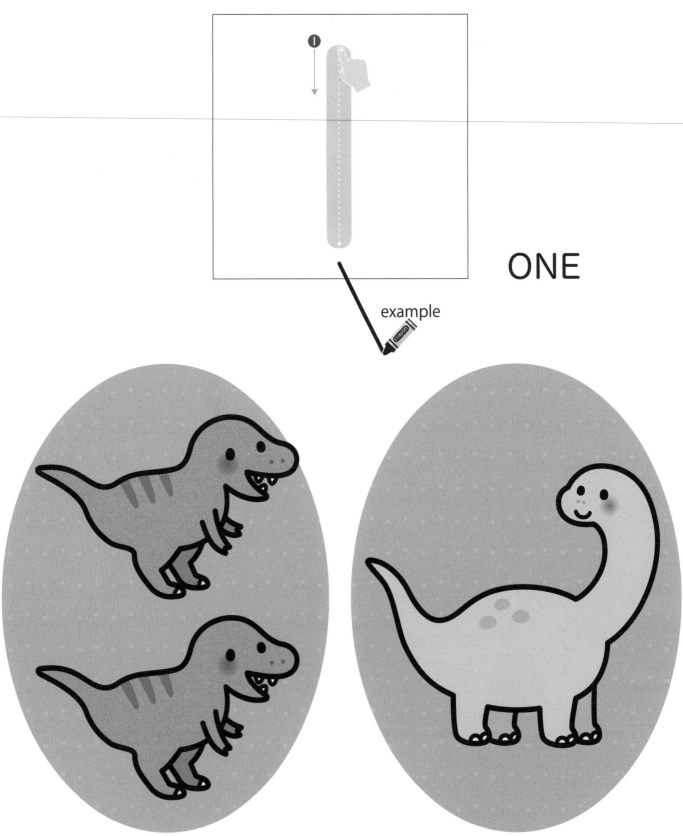

Trace and Match

To Parents: Encourage your child to trace the number 2 with a finger, then with a crayon. Count the giraffes in each piece of art to determine which matches the number 2. Be sure to ask, "Which piece of art has two giraffes?" Ask them to draw a line to the picture with 2 giraffes.

 Trace the number 2 and say "two." Then, draw a line to the pair of 2 animals.

TWO

Trace and Match

To Parents: Encourage your child to trace the number 3 with a finger, then with a crayon. Count the penguins in each piece of art to determine which matches the number 3. Be sure to ask, "Which piece of art has three penguins?" Ask them to draw a line to the picture with 3 penguins.

Trace the number 3 and say "three." Then, draw a line to the group of 3 animals.

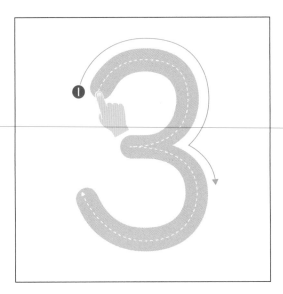

THREE

Trace and Match

To Parents: Encourage your child to trace the number 4 with a finger, then with a crayon. Count the turtles in each piece of art to determine which matches the number 4. Be sure to ask, "Which piece of art has four turtles?" Ask them to draw a line to the picture with 4 turtles.

Sticker

Good job!

 Trace the number 4 and say "four." Then, draw a line to the group of 4 animals.

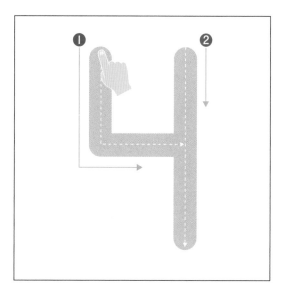

FOUR

Trace and Match

To Parents: Encourage your child to trace the number 5 with a finger, then with a crayon. Count the helicopters in each piece of art to determine which matches the number 5. Be sure to ask, "Which piece of art has five helicopters?" Ask them to draw a line to the picture with 5 helicopters.

  Trace the number 5 and say "five." Then, draw a line to the group of 5 vehicles.

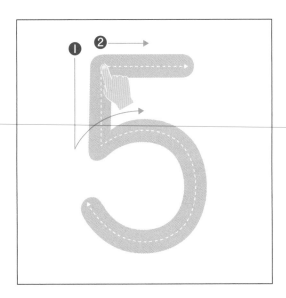

FIVE

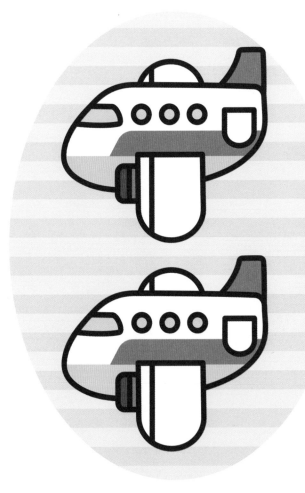

Match the Numbers

To Parents: First, cut the sweets along the solid gray lines. Next, count the sweets on each card together with your child. Before applying glue, encourage your child to place each card next to the number it corresponds with.

 Count the sweets on each card. Then, glue each card next to the number that matches the number of sweets.

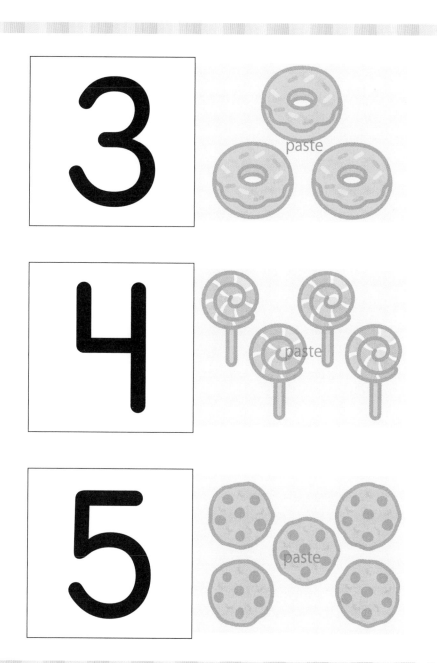

Parents: Cut out the sweets for your child.

Draw Using the Number 1

To Parents: Say to your child, "Let's think of something shaped like the number one, such as a pencil or a crayon." Have fun brainstorming together!

 Draw to turn the number 1 into something that is the same shape.

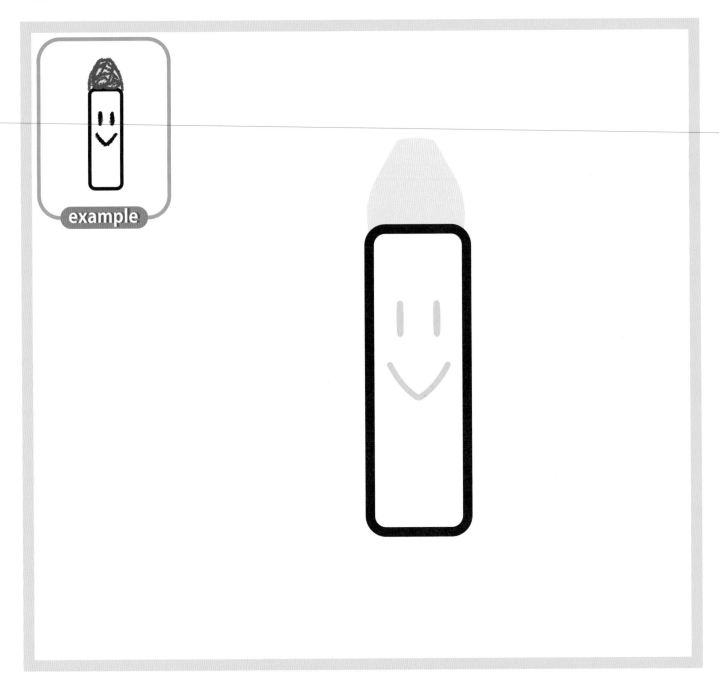

example

glue

glue

glue

Draw Using the Number 2

To Parents: If this activity seems too difficult for your child, give them a clue to spark their imagination. Tell them, "It looks like a hanger." Or, "It looks like a snake." It's also fine to rotate the book!

 Draw to turn the number 2 into something that is the same shape.

example

Use on page 34.

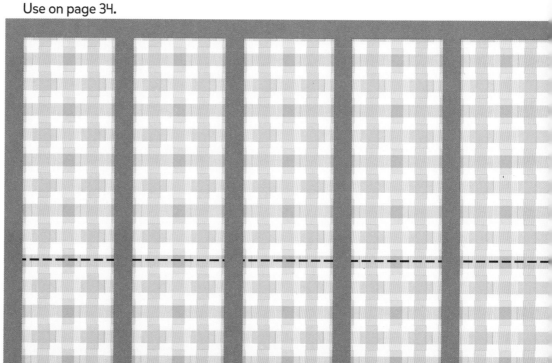

Play a Card Game

To Parents: Prepare the deck of cards for your child by cutting out the strips of paper and folding them as marked. Demonstrate how to play, following the directions below. Keep these cards handy to play on the go!

  Choose a card. Say the number on the card. Clap your hands the same number of times. Repeat with the other cards.

How to Play

① Cut out and fold as shown for your child.

② Pinch the folded section.

Fold

Take one!

3.

③ Let your child pick a card.

1, 2, 3.

Clap three times. 1, 2, 3.

④ Say and clap the number on the card. Take turns.

Parents: Cut out the cards for your child.

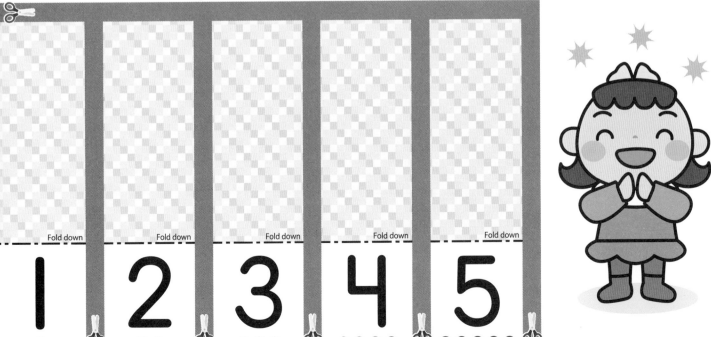

Fold down   Fold down   Fold down   Fold down   Fold down

1   2   3   4   5

Stand Like a Flamingo

To Parents: Stand next to your child and cross your right leg behind your left. Ask them to do the same to make their own number 4. You can take a picture so they can see what they look like.

Sticker
Good job!

 Trace the flamingo's legs with your finger. Then, cross your right leg behind your left to make the number 4.

More or Less?

To Parents: This activity focuses on volume comparison. Start by cutting and folding the page. Then, alternate between saying "more" and "less" as your child folds and unfolds the page. This will teach them "more" and "less." If your child doesn't understand, ask them to count both stacks of pancakes.

Repeat folding and unfolding the page. How does the number of pancakes change?

How to Play

Parents: Cut along the gray line for your child.

Bigger or Smaller?

To Parents: This activity focuses on size comparison. Cut and fold the page for your child. Talk to them about how the size of the pizza changes, introducing the words "bigger" and "smaller."

Repeat folding and unfolding the page. How does the pizza change?

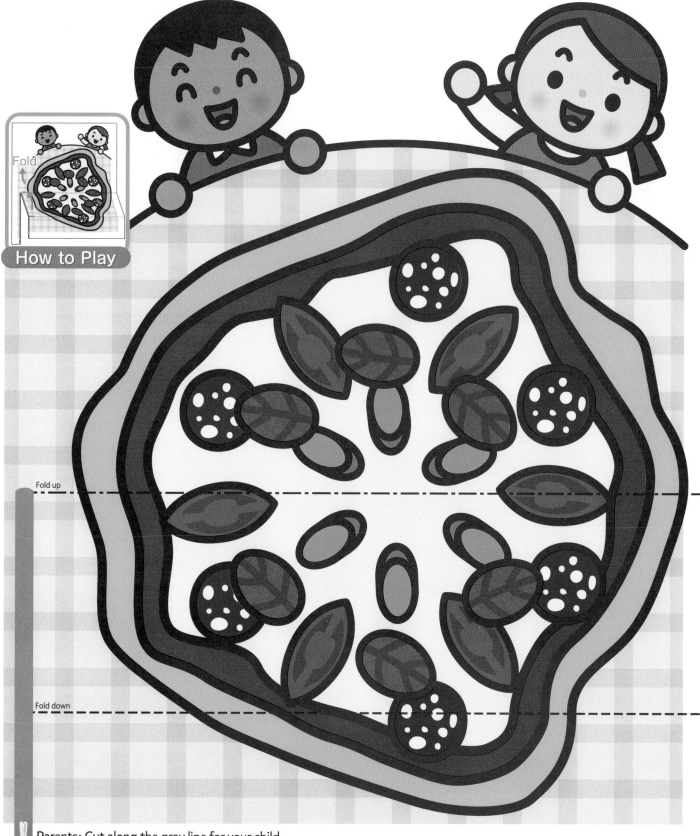

Fold

How to Play

Fold up

Fold down

Parents: Cut along the gray line for your child.

38

Which Is More?

To Parents: Your child may visually recognize which quantity is more without counting the fish. Let them also try deciding which group has more with objects in their daily life, such as crayons or toys.

 Color the ◯ under the tank that has more fish.

Which Is Bigger?

To Parents: This activity focuses on size comparison. Have your child hold their hands up against your own. Talk about "bigger" and "smaller."

 Which shirt is bigger? Color the ◯ under the bigger shirt.

Longer and Shorter

To Parents: This activity focuses on length comparison. Cut and fold the page for your child. Then, talk about the length of the lollipop stick. Introduce the words "longer" and "shorter" while folding and unfolding the page.

Repeat folding and unfolding the page. How does the lollipop stick change?

Fold

How to Play

Fold up

Fold down

Parents: Cut along the gray line for your child.

More and Less

Repeat folding and unfolding the page. How does the amount of juice change?

How to Play

Fold up

Fold down

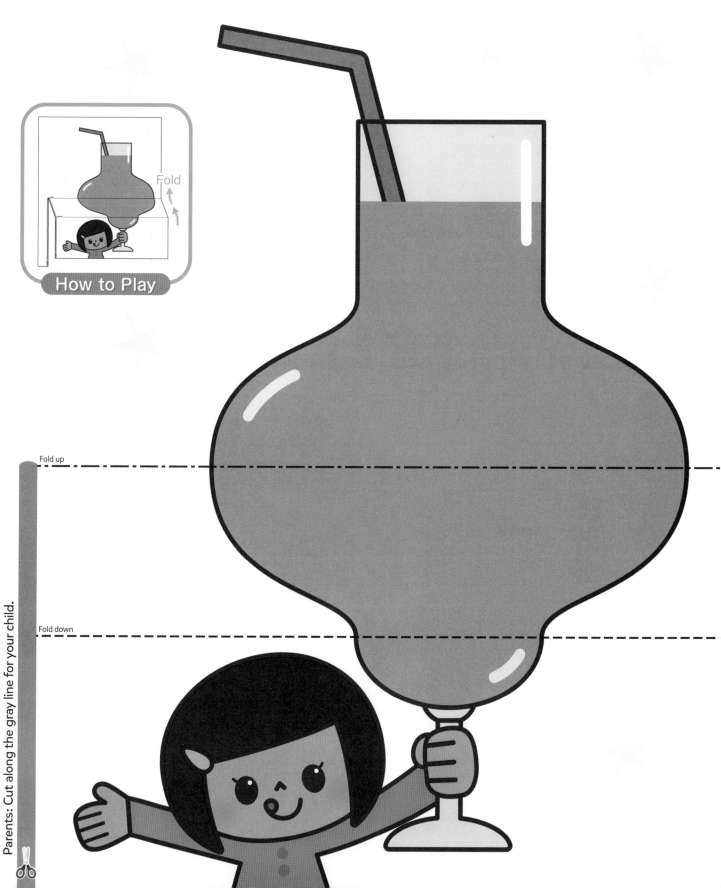

Which Is Longer?

To Parents: This activity focuses on length comparison. Show your child the end of each train. Then, compare which train is longer and which is shorter.

 Color the ◯ next to the longer train.

Which Is More?

To Parents: This activity focuses on volume comparison. Tell your child the milk bottles are the same size. It's also good to try pouring two glasses of milk to show your child a physical example of more and less.

 Color the ⭕ under the bottle that has more milk.

Draw Using a Circle

To Parents: Take turns tracing the shape of the circle with a finger and saying "circle." A smiley face is only one example of something that's shaped like a circle. Look around and talk about other examples, such as a ball, an orange, or a plate.

 Turn this ◯ into anything you like. You can draw a smiley face if you want.

example

CIRCLE

Draw Using a Square and a Triangle

To Parents: Begin by tracing and naming each shape. Then, look around for things that are shaped like squares and triangles, such as a truck or a window. Have fun brainstorming together!

Turn the ☐ and the △ into anything you like. You can draw faces on the shapes if you want.

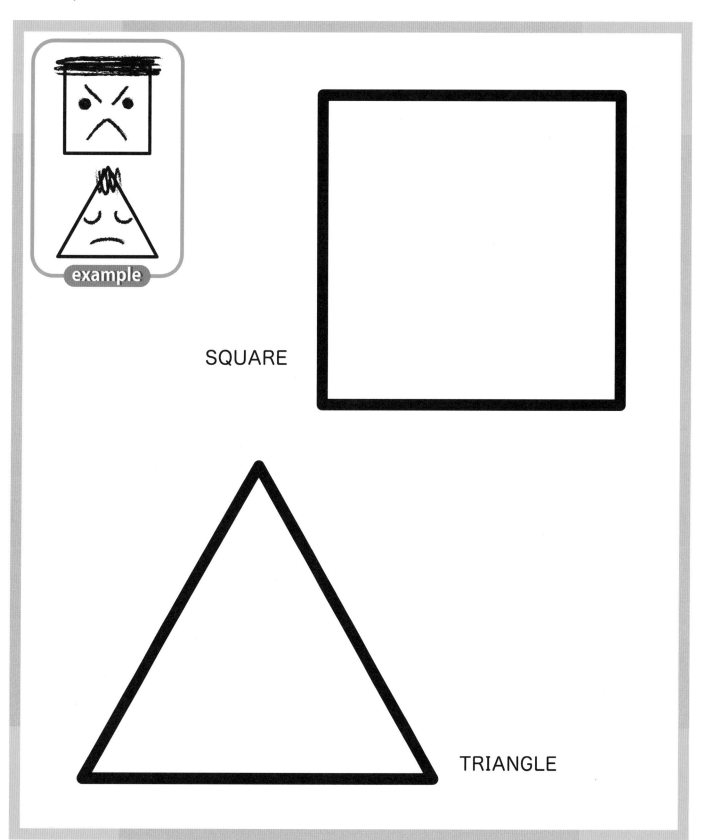

example

SQUARE

TRIANGLE

Fold to Make New Shapes

Good job!
Sticker

Can you guess what 2 shapes the monster will become? Fold the page to find out!

Fold

How to Play

Fold down

Fold up

Fold to Make New Shapes

To Parents: Can you and your child guess what shapes the monster will make when it's folded? Have fun trying. Then, fold the page for your child and see if you were right.

Sticker

★ Good job! ★

 Can you guess what 2 shapes the monster will become? Fold the page to find out!

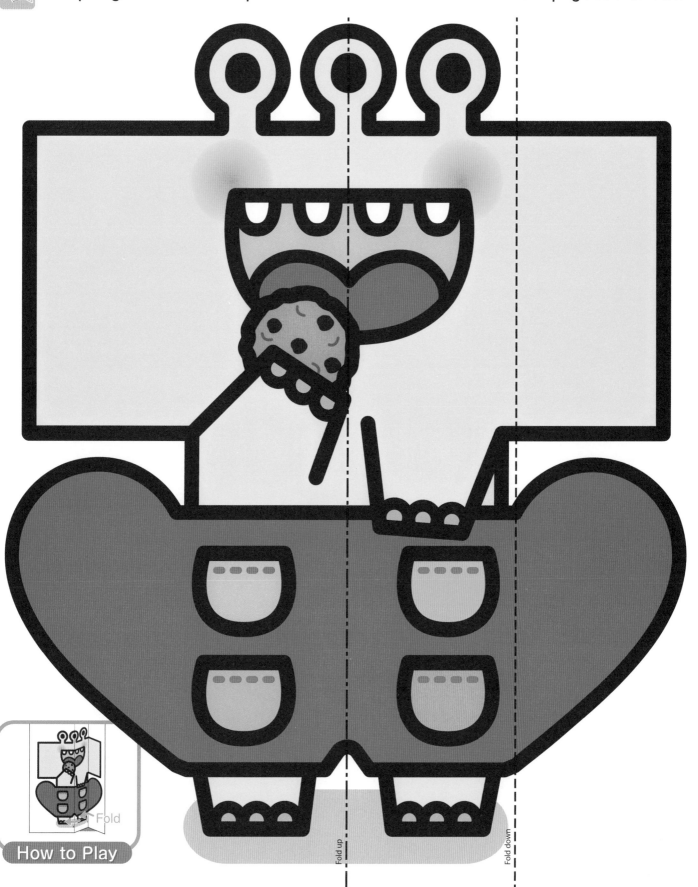

Fold up

Fold down

Fold

How to Play

Search and Find Shapes

To Parents: If your child is having difficulty, support them by asking them to say the shape of the sun, roof, and house. Give them the chance to search and find each shape in the picture, one at a time.

Can you name the 3 shapes at the bottom of the page? Draw a line to connect each shape to the same shape in the picture.

example

Match the Shapes

To Parents: Cut out the shapes at the bottom of the page and give them to your child. Help your child name the shapes and position them properly over the drawing. Then, let them place the shapes on the page after you apply the glue.

Place 2 animal faces on the page. Can you name both shapes?

TRIANGLE

paste

SQUARE

paste

CIRCLE

HEART

Parents: Cut out the faces for your child.

Follow the Number Path

To Parents: Model tracing with your finger, counting as you go. Then, encourage your child to do the same. Provide a crayon so your child can then trace the path.

  Trace the path in 1 → 2 → 3 order. Then, put a butterfly sticker on each flower.

Follow the Number Path

To Parents: Cut and fold the train cars for your child. Encourage them to count and trace the path with their finger. Then, take turns running the train along the path, saying, "one, two, three," as you go.

 Run the train along the track in 1 → 2 → 3 → 4 → 5 order.

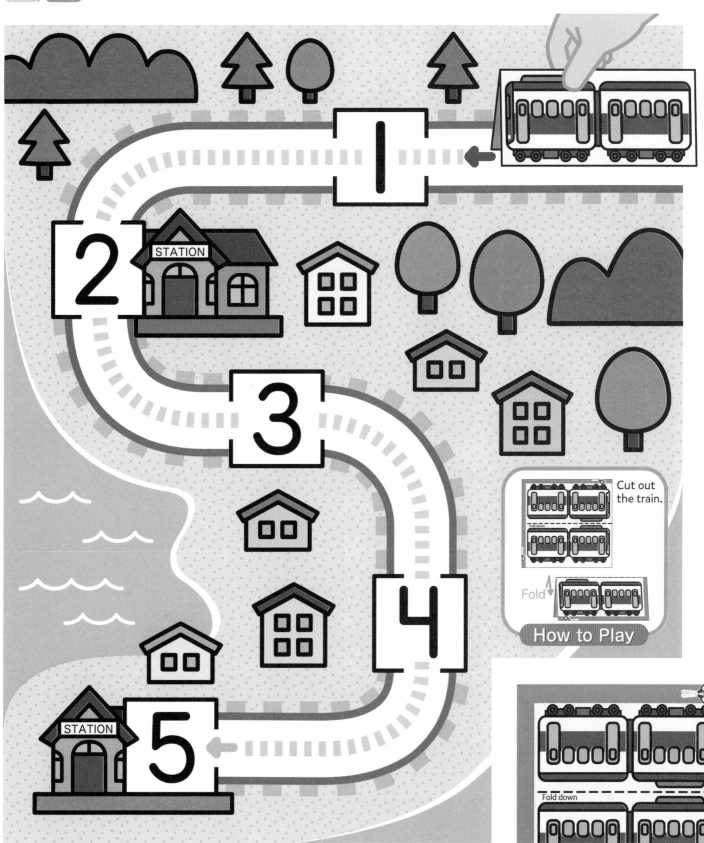

Cut out the train.

How to Play

Parents: Cut out the train for your child.

Connect the Dots

To Parents: Start by counting aloud from 1 to 5 with your child. Then, trace from dot to dot with a finger as you count. You may guide your child's hand when they try with a crayon.

Connect the dots from ● to ● in 1 → 2 → 3 → 4 → 5 order.

Connect the Dots

To Parents: Count aloud from 1 to 10 with your child. Then, trace from dot to dot with a finger as you count. You may guide your child's hand when they try with a crayon.

Sticker

★ Good job! ★

 Connect the dots from ● to ● in order from 1 to 10.

Match Numbers and Objects

To Parents: Point to and name the numbers with your child. In this activity, your child will practice finding numbers within a picture and increase their ability to recognize the shapes of numbers.

 Find 1, 2, and 3 in the picture. Then, draw a line to connect the matching number pairs.

example

Match Numbers and Objects

To Parents: Point to and name the numbers with your child. In this activity, your child will practice finding numbers within a picture and increase their ability to recognize the shapes of numbers. Finding a number within a picture develops attention and observation skills.

Find 4 and 5 in the picture. Then, draw a line to connect the matching number pairs.

example

Find the Number Match

To Parents: Start by counting the objects together. Then, encourage your child to draw a line connecting each number to the corresponding number of sweets.

Connect each number with the matching number of sweets.

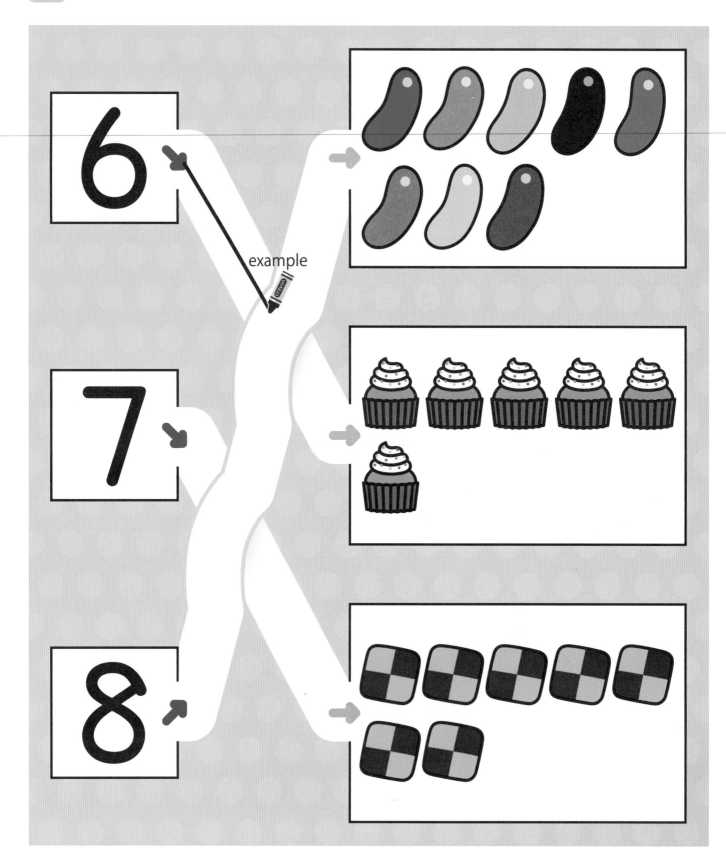

example

Find the Number Match

To Parents: Start by counting the objects together. Then, encourage your child to draw a line connecting each number to the corresponding number of desserts.

 Connect each number with the matching number of desserts.

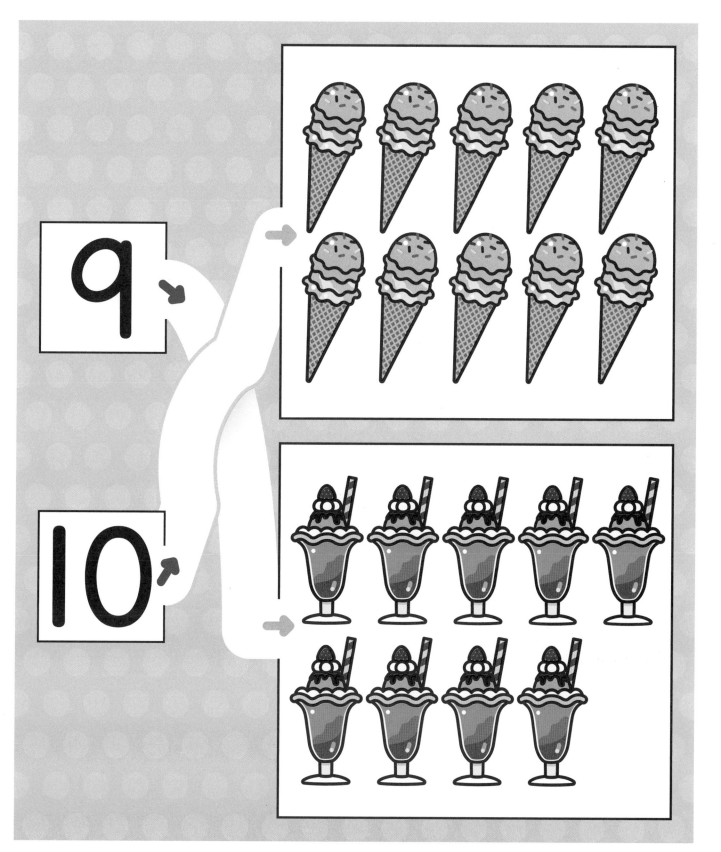

Play with Number Cards

To Parents: Cut out the cards on pages 59-64. There are countless ways to have fun and learn with number cards. Get inspired by the suggestions illustrated below, but let your child invent their own card games, too.

  There are many ways to play with the cards. Have fun!

Let's Make Pairs

1. Spread out 2 sets of cards numbered 1 through 5 (10 cards).

※ Master 1-5, then add more pairs to challenge your child.

2. Ask your child to make 5 matching pairs.

Match the same numbers!

2 and 2!

Let's Count

※ Master 1-5, then add more numbers to challenge your child.

1. Create a deck of 5 cards numbered 1 through 5. Together, count the objects pictured on each card.

2. Shuffle the deck and show the picture side to your child. Then, ask your child to count the objects on each card. After your child counts, flip the card to show the corresponding number.

1, 2, 3.   *1, 2, 3.*

Let's count!   *1, 2, 3.*   *You did it!*

Arrange Numbers

1. Put cards 1 through 5 on the table in order. Then, spread out a second set of cards, 1 through 5, and ask your child to put them in order under your example cards.

2. Next time, remove your example cards. Spread out cards 1 through 5. Now ask your child to put the cards in order again.

※ Master 1-5, then add more numbers to challenge your child.

1, 2...

More and Less

1. Show your child the picture side of 2 different cards.

2. Ask, "Which card has more objects?" and "Which card has less?"

Which has more?

This one!

Make a Card Case

Find and cut out the card case on page 63. Follow this diagram to fold it.

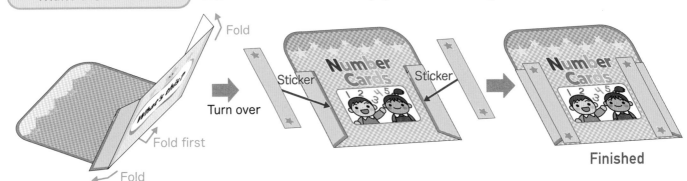

Fold

Turn over

Sticker   Sticker

Fold first

Fold

Finished

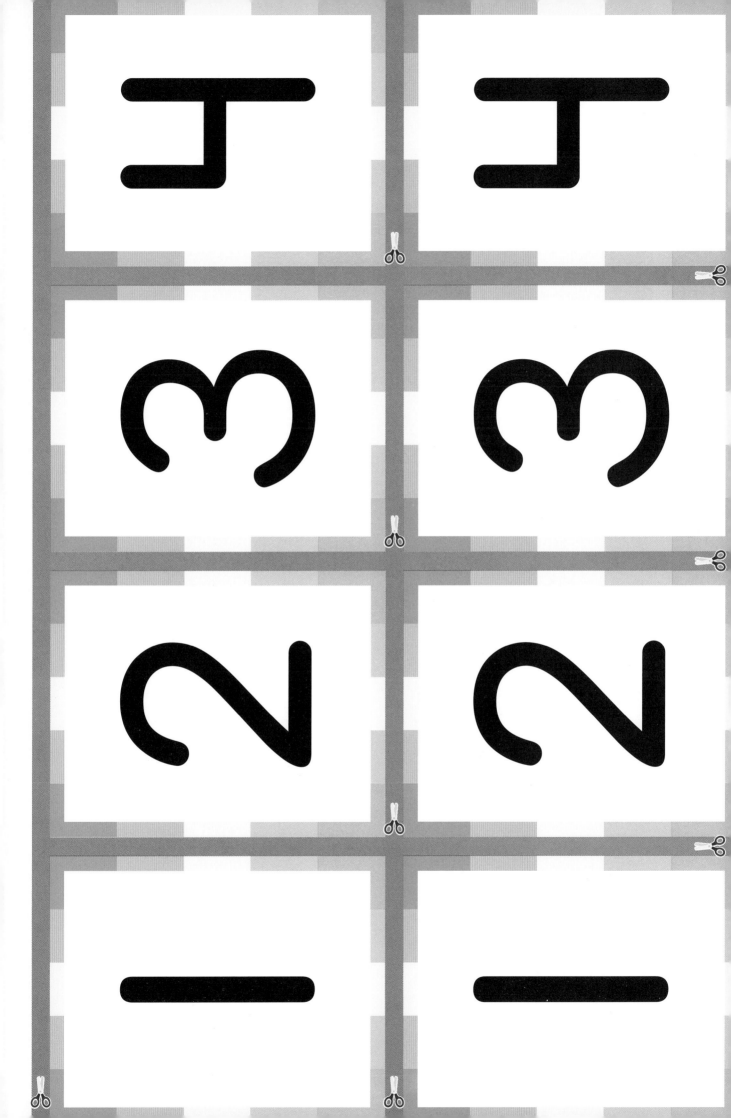

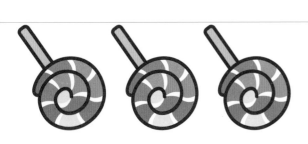

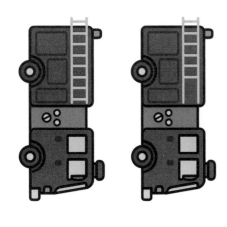

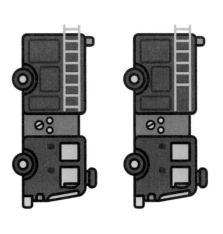

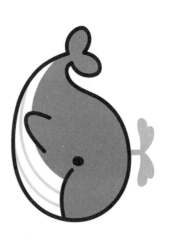

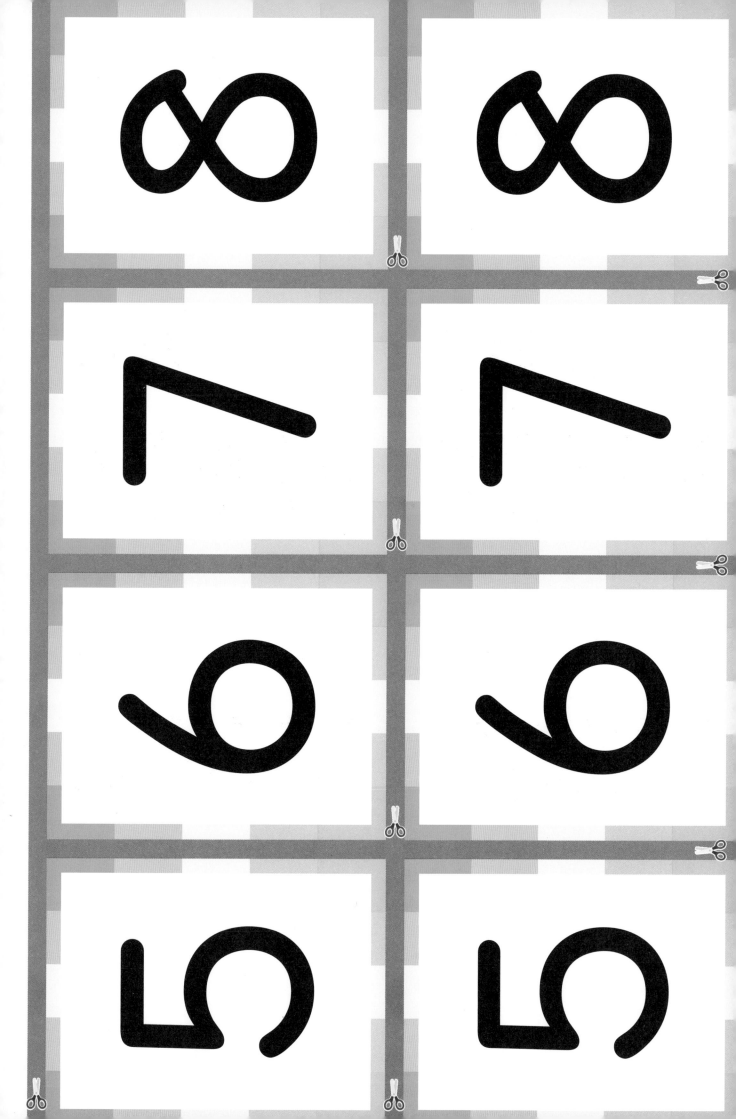

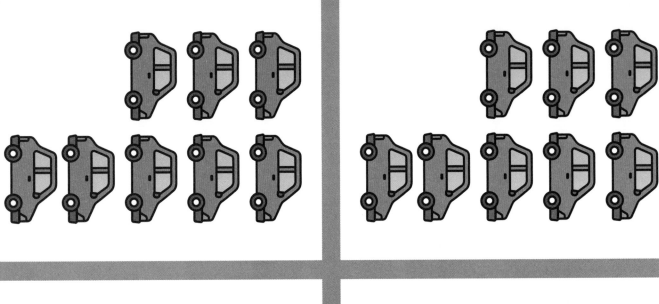

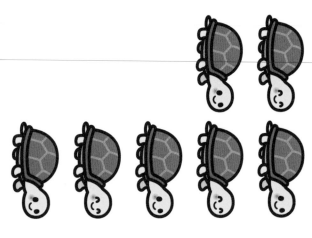

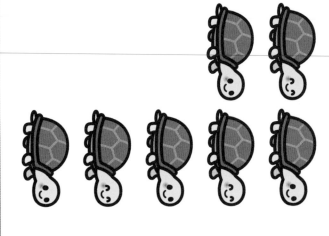

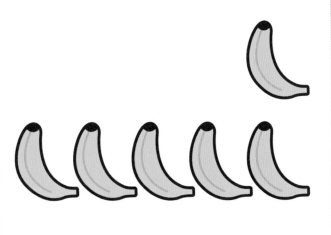

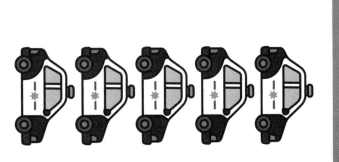

O I

O I

q

b

2

Number Cards

1 2 3 4 5

Card Holder

1

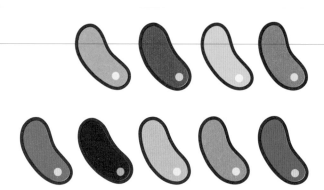

2

1

WIPE-CLEAN Numbers Board

Let's write the numbers by tracing the lines.

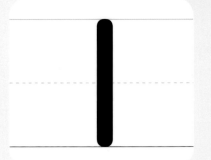
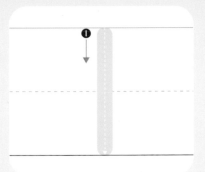

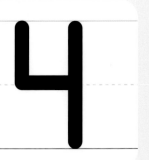
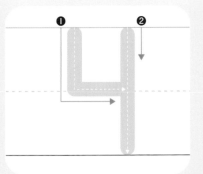
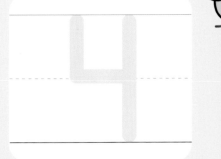

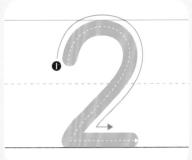

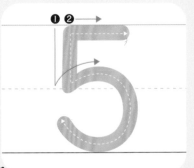

1 2 3 4 5